Some Trick Of Light

For you, Karen —
Appreciating you, your
spirit, your teaching style,
your writing. Thank you.
Fondly,
Jane Glazer
Cannon Beach 8/2/00

Some Trick Of Light

Poems by Jane Glazer

ADRIENNE LEE PRESS

ISBN 0-962914-2-x.

Adrienne Lee Press
An imprint of *Calapooya Collage*
Thomas L. Ferté, Editor and Publisher
Post Office Box 309
Monmouth, Oregon 97361

Acknowledgments

Thanks are due to the following periodicals in which many of these poems were first published: *Antioch Review,* "Some Trick of Light;" *Bellowing Ark,* "Fireflies of Italy," "Short Rations," "Stomping Out the Blues" (formerly titled "Out of the Same Pajamas"), "To Other Worlds," "Vanishing Point," "Veterinarian's Daughter," "We Will Build a Fire Now," "Woman Carrying Plum Blossoms;" *Berkeley Poetry Review,* "Whispers from Guatemala;" *Calapooya Collage,* "At Walden Pond," "Conjugal Ghost," "The Cowl of Night," "Deirdre," "In the Waterfall Garden: Seattle," "Parrot on Fire," "Rounding the Figures," "Small Graves," "St. Grandma, the Baptist," "Widower;" *Calyx,* "Final Disposition," "Point of No Return;" *Central American Update,* "Las Palomas de Paz;" *Fireweed,* "As If to Say," "Beside a Desert River," "Going Underground;" *Five-Fingers Review,* "The Diagonal Path;" *Hubbub,* "Drink of the Cup;" *Chester H. Jones,* "Short Notice;" *Mid-American Review,* "Mother's Mother;" *O.C.T.E. Journal,* "If Your Hands;" *Plainswoman,* "The Harvester;" *Raven Chronicles,* "Ceremonial Rites;" *Sojourner,* "Suicide;" *Tree Connections,* "Heartwood;" *Willamette Week,* "Museum Exhibit."

"Call the Interval Happiness" originally appeared in *Stafford's Road,* Adrienne Lee Press, 1991.

To Howard
—for the gift of love

Contents

I. The Endlessness of Stars

As If To Say   *3*

Whispers from Guatemala   *4*

Rounding the Figures   *6*

Las Palomas de Paz   *8*

Slaughterhouse in Venezuela   *9*

The Diagonal Path   *10*

Vanishing Point   *12*

Deirdre   *14*

The Fireflies of Italy   *15*

Some Trick of Light   *16*

Maybe Made in Kiev   *18*

The Hutongs of Beijing   *20*

Woman Carrying Plum Blossoms   *21*

Teahouse Jazz   *22*

Ceremonial Rites   *24*

Museum Exhibit   *26*

We Will Build a Fire Now   *27*

II. Into the Seaward River

Mother's Mother   *31*

Final Disposition   *32*

Small Graves   *33*

Suicide   *34*

Short Notice   *36*

If Your Hands   *37*

Stomping Out the Blues   *38*

The Cowl of Night   *40*

St. Grandma the Baptist   *41*

Veterinarian's Daughter   *42*

Parrot on Fire   *44*

Signal Flowers   *46*

Going Underground   *48*

To Other Worlds   *49*

Different Albums   *50*

Dawn Wind   *52*

Winter Wake for My Brother   *54*

III. At the Edge of the Land

Drink of the Cup   *59*

The Harvester   *60*

Point of No Return   *62*

Heartwood   *64*

Beside a Desert River   *65*

Conjugal Ghost   *66*

Short Rations   *68*

In the Waterfall Garden: Seattle   *70*

At Walden Pond   *71*

Call the Interval Happiness   *72*

Wheat Harvest   *74*

Widower   *76*

Evening Light   *77*

I

The Endlessness of Stars

As If To Say

on "Vegetal Evil," by Paul Klee

Riveting as a puzzle in a children's magazine—
    (find the squirrel, the owl, the witch)—
the red room shrinks down into a tangling
net of vines, into Paul Klee's fantasy.
      Bewitched by pen and ink, fine lines
of twisted bittersweet, its fleshy,
orange arils, I move in
      close to stare.

Shapes ensnare—greenbrier, wild oat, bindweed;
    spines like dandelion seeds
fly from flower stamens; a spadix fallen
to the ground, tethered by arms of eel grass;
      tongues of foxfires licking rotted wood.
Seductive legs of lilies, lascivious
as seaweed, wrap the jungle roots
      emerging from the water.

Think of quicksand, screened
    by ligneous vines and undergrowth,
of fugitives hiding in the bayou.
Imagine the artist, looking at these
      spidered lines, trying to title a sketch
so finely drawn it webs the surface
and the sinister together, as if to say
things have two sides:
      artifice on top, the truth just under.

Whispers from Guatemala

We cannot make it to San Cristobal.
The vines are thick, and monkeys tattle.
Guards patrol the train tracks out of Tenosique,
and old Mateo told me they have sunk
our log canoes along the river.

In Lago Ts'ibatnah, three bloated bodies,
headless, float in the reeds.
Whatever path we take is full of danger,
mi hermana, but I will guide you,
you and Koh Maria, K'ayum and Nuk.

Lying beside you, I listen for the tree roots,
for the corn God, stirring. They are silent.
Here, outside Huehuetenango, the leaves
hang heavy with cold night dew,
but we must hide till morning.

The mists are shifting. There is little time.
Tomorrow, I can take the baby for you
longer. This year, our *milpa* was not planted
and without the squash and beans,
my knees are weak, my belly rumbles.

I should make a pilgrimage to Naha,
but the jungle way is long.
I am afraid. The Gods are hiding,
too, outside their houses.
The incense pots are cold.

I have wrapped inside my *manta* two tortillas;
eat one before the Sun sends us his light.
Ask permission of the corn, first,
so the keeper of the path goes with us.

Do not make quick moves, Chan K'in says,
or they will see the colors of your shawl.
The Brute Ones practice shooting
orchids, bananas, the bright green quetzal.

Rounding the Figures

The newborns lie along both walls
in this oblong room, four to a wooden box,
helpless hatchlings fallen from the nest,
shrunken skin sacks in the throes of death.

Their mewlings are as weak as air
through hollow straw. Diapers rise
around them like bread dough. Their heels
draw back to kick the alien air

while fists of birdbone clutch the reins
of breath. Above their folded shoulders,
each head, a thick, black cap of hair—
mothballed chickadees in museum drawers.

Dr. Rada, Head of Pediatrics, tells me
these will die, all, of malnutrition,
gastroenteritis, twenty or thirty—
he rounds the figures—every week.

My chest constricts with disbelief
I can't explain—a mother's grief?
The shrine in *La Parroquia* swims in my eyes,
the heat of votive candles, the wavering Virgin.

Nine months of waiting over, sad-eyed
mothers, their breasts swollen, dripping milk,
will bend to whitewash tiny coffins
hammered out of salvage for these *angelitos*.

Outside the window it is spring and nesting time.
The ravens caw across the canyons to each other.
They pull apart the Spanish moss that drapes
like graveclothes from *guayabo* trees.

Las Palomas de Paz

for David and Elisabeth Linder

May Day in Portland, all bees
and rhododendrons, the *Flor de Sacauanjoche,*
Nicaraguan Folkloric Dancers,
celebrated Ben. Their director,
his friend, Rosalina Moreno,
spoke of his brief life, his bravery,
enjoined us not to grieve
but to applaud his spirit, to think
not of the grave but of the resurrection.
"We do not ask for a moment of silence,"
she told us in soft Spanish,
"we want a moment of applause!"

And then, the auditorium packed,
chairs blocking all the aisles,
that huge audience exploded, our hands
clapping Ben back home.
    Pallbearers carried his small body
to its rest in Matagalpa, but we were juggling
his soul, so huge and light it seemed a beach ball
or a circus balloon we could reach together,
keeping it afloat there in that room.

In the din that tried to match
his spirit, a mirage of tears
transformed the hands to wings,
white wings of hope that beat
against the night, the doves of peace
that Ben has set in flight.

Slaughterhouse in Venezuela

Vultures along the roof ridge wait.
Anything can die here. Pigs scream in the pens,
the coppery smell of blood and butchers' gore
hose past them to a last entrapment.
These birds know where to look for carrion.

Outside El Vigia, the slaughterhouse is new,
a source of civic pride in this Andean town.
We have been brought to see it, to admire.
The surfaces inside gleam cold white tile.
Stripped of hide, the red sawn halves of beef

steam on stainless trolley rails.
The just-killed animals do not give up quickly.
Flesh quivers on the carcasses, the dumb cells
jerk. Living muscles, brutally assailed,
twitch against the stunning bolt, refuse to die.

Dull-eyed, the men inside lug hoses.
They work all night slaughtering these cattle,
in smocks, once white, blood-wet on shoulders
and sleeves now, splattered to the boots.
Each butcher wears an arsenal of cutlery

around his waist—flayer, sticker,
splitter, slicer—the steel clanking
on chains like jailer's keys. They own them.
They are proud of these. The sharpest knife
hangs down in front, kept in a leather sheath.

The Diagonal Path

How fragile here
under the agitated trees,
the locust and the rubber shushing,
rustling together
in the Nicaraguan night,
the sprinkler's *pock-pock*
searching out banana leaves.

And it is quiet, too,
despite the argument
of tree frogs and cicadas,
the dark somehow suspended.
From the bomb-shattered church
across the road, where pigeons
slanting before the open nave
make candles flicker,
where a dog hunts holy crumbs,
so hunger-thin his ribs
rake shadows up the aisle,
a children's choir practices
for *Navidad,* their creche
a cardboard manger filled
with Spanish moss.

Ceremony and the season
teach us to let the night suffice,
to feel the instability of air,
the endlessness of stars.

Down the hill,
outlined against the fading light,
a woman walks,
the path diagonal,
her lantern swinging
to the rhythm of her need.

Vanishing Point

Two hours and fifty cents out of La Paz,
at Tiahuanaco, where the Andes bend
their bony knees into Bolivia,
everything is thin. The air is thin,
the soup we find to eat is thin,
served by thin, raspberry-skinned
children with thin hands.
We have come to see the ruins
of the birthplace of the sun,
here on the Altiplano,
once-pregnant bowl, fleshless now,
hollowed out like pelvic bones.

Beyond the village, among sheep
grazing on dry tundra, the huge carved stones,
crude megaliths, flank the gate
through which the sun escaped.
What prodigious labor, on oxygen's
half-ration, moved them, and from where?
Suddenly, a bicycle is born.
Everything is brown—the puffs of dust,
the alien machine, the boy turning up
from the crumbling town like a Tarot card,
a trick dealt by this rare air.

He skids to a stop, hops off,
holds out to us a burlap bag of bones.
We know about instant history,

the life he tries, but buy
his old sheep's knuckle anyway,
smelling on his clothes
the charring fire that aged it,
the parings from his mother's knife.
Radiant, he turns back home,
then disappears, lifts off
the earth without a trace of
wheels, bones, wisp of hair.

Deirdre

Old Deirdre hid herself in copses,
lying down at sunset in ditches of brassy water,
beds with sheets of gold unfurled for her,
she thought, on the edge of the edge of the world.
People say she wandered from the convent
after forty years, to roam the roads
of rural Ireland, through the rocks, fog,
bogs of that wild heath without a hearth
or kettle she could call her own.

Her white hair, frayed as rope, haloed her face
like the aureole around Saint Kevin.
She begged for food that wouldn't hurt her teeth,
called all bread unleavened,
said it was the Eucharist. She ate rose hips,
raw eggs and stolen fruits. From gardens
in the moonlight she dug up roots,
meandered into town on market days.

Always looking for something lost, she stared
across the water, asking anyone who dared to speak
to her where Cyprus was. Her sea-green eyes
followed in any direction, her cracked lips
trembled; in fantasy, she saw a land
where sun burned through clear light,
where the moon in a manger of stars
rocked through the night. She dreamed
of doing penance there, where Christ stopped,
of lying down in an olive press,
not in these dank woods where the black rooks,
crying distress, circled above the trees.

The Fireflies of Italy

Halfway between Perugia and Assisi,
a gas pump, a crunch of eggshell houses
cluster in a field, stone-poor,
gone to grass. We stop to stretch,
to check the map, to breathe
the unadulterated air of sunset.
Twenty centuries of Etruscan bone dust
moulder here, in crypts hacked out of rock.
From the village, a small bell
rings the Angelus, cracked, off-key.

In among the grass heads as suddenly
as summoned, fireflies blink on, their wiry
bodies bits of tinder in the coppery
twilight. Thousands at once—millions
maybe—chips of glazed terra cotta
mirroring the sky flame. Coded messages
flash, *da da dit, dit da,* intermittent
orange, floating sparks above
the burned-out straw.

Crows caw in the nightfall over this hard
umber earth, this clay pre-Roman stuccoes
once were made of. All the shattered
lives, their histories, rekindle. Energies
catch fire again, pulsing the mystery
through twisted cypress trees.

Some Trick of Light

Along the reservoir,
the old, wrought-iron fence
      is white with rime.
By some trick of light, Anna Akhmatova,
whose poems I am reading, suddenly appears,
the way Modigliani painted her in Paris,
      or walking in St. Petersburg in 1910.

Under a fringed shawl,
wool challis splashed with roses,
      her long skirt slaps
against black boot tops as she strides
like ink across a page, her chin defying
all those grievous years. Then,
she slips into history, disappears
      in this honest air. Just bones remain.

Beside the gardens, a mound of sawdust,
whitened like a shroud by recent snow,
      becomes her grave. I stop there,
in a ghost of my own breathing,
to praise her simple fire,
spare as a wooden match
      flickering against the cold.

I think of the courage of women,
      how they endure,
how they walk miles to carry back water,

silence their pain, apportion
what's left of the rice.
    Keepers of eggs without shells,
they know how fragile the days are,
        how hope can spill into the ground.

Maybe Made in Kiev

When I was so much earth
    and starlight, willow tree and wind,
I dreamed of leaning over the bluff's edge
into that updraft of air,
       of flying across the world,
myself a magic carpet, or like Nils,
    on the back of a goose,

looking for mother's tea-cozy
brought to her from Russia,
    maybe made in Kiev or in Samarkand,
some land I'd never seen,
a plum chintz and kapok-skirted
      babushka I talked to
and whose puff-sleeved blouse I washed,
    hung up with dolly clothespins.

Maybe in Tbilisi, magic name, a spell
of spires, gold onion domes,
    wild Caucasian music!
      I have only been to Sitka,
Russian toehold in the new world.
Even there, Slavic and mysterious,
    the salmon, the eagles,
the spruce on Mt. Verstovia.
    I want to come to you, now,

to see the turquoise river, Kura,
blue with gold stars sparkling,
    icons, hand-hewn rafters under tile.

Samovar of mystery,
I come to drink from glass teacups
　　　ornate with filigree.
Roll out your ancient carpet,
　　　hand me a sandalwood fan.

The Hutongs of Beijing

Slits of sun filter through fig leaves
in a courtyard where braids of garlic
in rows like lengths of rope
are laid to dry. Canaries titter,
their bamboo cages hung low in the branches.
In this year of the snake, old men
whose reptilian faces miss nothing,
hiss together in the dappled afternoon.

Glazed dragon scales snake across the tops
of mud walls, a few tiles missing now,
like teeth from elders, all along
the hutongs, narrow alleys eeling through
Beijing, concave with age but wide enough
     for one bicycle piled with eggplant,
          three chickens,
               two grandmothers, gossiping,
unaware of time. It could be centuries ago,
or yesterday, in dust or monsoon mud.

A girl with long hair, black as lacquer,
her duck eggs in a wicker basket,
counts them out for a white-haired woman
with stubbed feet, her oval shoes
no bigger than the eggs she bargains for.
They squat beside a moongate, dickering,
their voices quick, sharp as serpents' teeth,
spitting out the seeds of compromise.

Woman Carrying Plum Blossoms

By Safeway, between crocus time
and lilacs, when first plum blossoms
shock the season white, an umbrella of branches
hunches across the street against the light,
oblivious to traffic, heading toward
an old, downtown hotel.

A snail of a woman in flat, cotton shoes,
her trunk padded in a lavender quilted coat,
clutches an explosion of flowering plum
from a tree she staked out weeks ago.
She steadies a broom of sticks
switching in air, almost as tall as she,
the broken stem ends bandaged in rags,
her hands bare.

A long, mulberry-colored shawl
cocoons her head in wool, hangs down her back
like a bruised braid. She passes,
her Chinese face crinkled as pongee,
her eyes dark plum pits,
her flesh, their yellow fruit.

Seeing me admire, her free hand
thumbs the winter scarf back off
her forehead. With few teeth left,
armed with harmony and unafraid,
she smiles—unbidden light, hidden
in rose jade.

Teahouse Jazz

Into this perfect air,
hovering between September and October,
    the jazz notes fall,
clear as water from a bamboo pipe,
the pool of twilight weightless and still.
The harmonies reverberate
        together, or alone, like
stepping stones that lead
    beneath deep eaves of this verandah.
        Two bronze lanterns
hum the music from the cantilevered roof.

The Yamaha piano, lacquer-black,
the double bass,
    its belly fat as Buddha's,
the high-hat cymbals of the drummer—
ancient temple gongs—
        beat the tempo for the scat
the singer moans,
    her eyes closed, against her hip
just one hand clapping.

Savor the sound set free
on this Pacific rim,
    the Japanese Gardens, moss
and contorted pine, raked gravel underfoot,
three stars above, the city
        coming on like fireflies.

Shoji screens and cedar poles
enclose the teahouse space,
        empty as the ends of song
carried on a breeze that rings
pagoda bells. West comes to East,
        or East to West,
                the difference
as delicate as split-leaf maple trees.

Ceremonial Rites

Elders Week comes to the Quileute
with a deerhide drum, a belt buckle
hammered out of car parts, and a tape
recorder. The old man, Black Bear,
believes in passing on the culture.
What he doesn't know is how to read
the signs kids do, in La Push or anywhere—
what to sing, what to smoke, what not to wear.

He tells his tales in a corrugated trailer
rusting by the quarry cliffs,
the tribal school a stone's throw
from the waves, its thin roof
amplifying rain which nearly drowns
his smoke-dry voice. The children
(to whom these tales belong, he says)
snap their satin jackets, pay no attention.

One girl, flat-chested, at most thirteen,
squeaks in her chair, bored with animal pelts
and amulets. She wears, cinched at the waist,
a homemade cotton dress, and on her feet
a pair of three-inch heels, sling pumps
of molded wood precarious as stilts,
her calfless legs a frame for pantyhose,
sagging behind the knees.

As Black Bear drones on, telling stories
of tribal braves, their famous deeds—

Hear Well, who listened to spiders,
Drink Well, who quaffed a whole lake—
she pouts out the window, restless,
points, unpoints her toes. She's seen T.V.,
longs to live a different life, as far
from moccasins as it is possible to be.

Museum Exhibit

on the sculpture of Magdelena Abakanowicz

Tons of coarsest jute,
tangled as elflock,
mold these mute and boneless shapes,
hunched-over, headless victims
of a firing squad, or corpses
bagged for flatbed trucks.

All that burlap, sutured
to the backs of hollow bodies,
smells of blisters broken,
of damp earth in spring,
sacks of shrivelled tubers snaking
from black rot in cellars.

Still, they sit, staring
without eyes, howling
without mouths, with such thin skin,
their ashen sackcloth stretched
to hold in shrapnel splinters
burst inside the mind.

The figures are drained,
cadaverous, the guts gone back
into the dark, the tears to rain,
the blood to viscous clay.
Only the shells remain,
the echoes of their crying.
    They should be gone.
    Dying should be the end of pain.

We Will Build a Fire Now

Richard A. Campbell, 1930-1985

The snow, seductive, twirls its gauze
around Thanksgiving. The cold is premature.
I turn my chair toward the garden
where the flakes fall thick,
remembering how, in China, beside the lotus ponds,
butterflies dance like snowflakes
in the morning glories.

I want the sky to suck it back;
I want to tell you, wait,
don't start your journey in dark weather.
Wait. How will those of us who knew you,
heard you belt out Beethoven's *Chorale,*
who puzzled over Housman, drowned
the Karamazov dialectic in red wine,
how will we find our way
without your light?

A Japanese ink wash now, the fir trees,
those sentinels across the valley,
are fading in the snowfall. Their spiny tops
soften with fine, gray shade.
Look how the snow curls white arms
around the boxwood.
We were not prepared for early cold.

II

Into the Seaward River

Mother's Mother

Ella Clementine Chantry, 1870-1966

It was hard to tell grandmother
from her stove. Both had legs
that bowed out at the knees,
a pilot light, and great ideas.
She loved to wrap her garbage
every night, a ritual she was bent
on teaching me. The supper dishes
done, pans back in the oven,
she unfolded old newspapers
kitty-corner on the stovetop,
heaped the peels and rinds
drained in the strainer
while we finished chores,
dead in the middle.

Then, like diapering a baby,
she folded the sides in smoothly,
packaging the mess into an envelope,
tidy as a Chinese New Year's toy.
When the sports page angled
on the final roll, she'd take
a rubber band down from the nail
beside the stove, twist it
into quarters and secure the whole.

I had to pack it neatly in the
battered can. They say she took
a fancy to the garbage man.

Final Disposition

Xela Chantry Belton, 1898-1974

Others divided closets full of mother's things.
From the earth, I took her poppies.
I wanted those fandango folds
of red and black chiffon she doted on,
loving the wild and Moorish music of them,
coating her tongue with the thin skin
of their crimson petals.

   Snapping her fingers, flamenco dancer,
   she'd mock the clack of castanets
   in answer to their gypsy cadence.
   She would crouch toward the flounce of flowers,
   twirl, stamp her foot, then kick it out
   as if to lift the ruffles, scarlet
   along the hemline of her yard.

And so, I dug up, soil and all,
the thistle-toothed and gray-green clumps
of leaves, the testicle seedpods and hairy stems
both out of season, to transplant them
in my less-exotic garden. There, they bloom
her blood's abandon, year after year,
roots holding, their poppy heads nodding
a carefree, opium-ecstatic, possibly forever sleep.

Small Graves

Last week, before a metal marker
on a grave in Oysterville,
I stopped to read the legend:
"Infant Daughter: 0 Yrs. 0 Mos. 0 Dys."
      How strange....
What drew me, questing all my days
for answers, to this small mound?

    And I was looking up at Daddy
    one Memorial Day, my arms stickered
    with yellow climber roses, beside
    a little grave in Redfield, Iowa.

There, I'd seen my own name,
written on the plate, in an oxidized
frame on a metal stake, where,
my father told me, their first baby,

    "your little sister," he called her, lay,
    already dead four years when I was born.
    "She had your name first," he said,
    "but barely lived a day."

I had never heard about their loss.
It made me lonely for them, then,
and still today, in Oysterville, I think
how irreconcilable, death at birth—
      strange other Jane.

How sad they must have been,
all those little clothes....

Suicide

John Hector McLean, 1925-1956

Her first thought had been to bring him presents,
to tell him goodbye, somehow, by giving them,
to hide her hurt that he would go this way.
In their bedside table she found his wedding ring,
put there for a last golf game—
    it always calloused his finger—
and a Christmas portrait of the kids
with Santa Claus, wallet size, and one of her,
so he might see, in whatever place
he woke up, how they used to be.

Like segments of a pearl string
scattered in a drawer, unopened for over
thirty years, her words spilled out,
the tears almost dry now, telling how,
on that day, her heart pounded,
her head shook no, no....
    On a slab in the morgue,
under a sheet draped crookedly across his knees,
she found him, contorted to the rigid contours
of the car where the trigger clicked,
the blue eyelids bulging, lips thick,
the whole head bruised from a temple wound
covered now with make-up,
petalled out like a full-blown flower.

She could not touch him.
She was afraid.

She could not now, and never had,
forgiven herself that withheld touch....
    But it was odd that he
didn't brush away the fly that crawled
from his pasty hair, that there was no echo
in that gray basement cave,
silent as the aftermath of avalanche,
his finger too swollen for the ring,
no place anywhere to put the pictures.

Short Notice

This deep lungful of country,
rock-ribbed and naked, heavy with sleep,
stumbles down to the water's edge,
collapses, draws its fetal knees
into position. Huge buttocks
and flanks, smooth as chamois,
sink into slumber. Creases of dark
crotch and armpits fill up with shadow.

Day's end pulls the salmony sky
into the seaward river. Against
the currents of wind and of water,
I hurry, past Rooster Rock,
Bridal Veil Falls, the burial ground
on Memaloose Island.

The wind, gasping for breath
as the gorge narrows,
throws whitecaps over the spindrift,
bowls tumbleweeds like pills
spilled from the tables of giants.

I am coming to Yakima, Daddy;
wait for me!

If Your Hands

Merrill Jesse Belton, 1896-1986

The sound in cold air
exploded like rifle shot
when I knocked on your coffin
that last January morning.
Two sharp raps on the lid—
a thing you might have done
to summon us for supper.

> Iowa winter dusks, in from the barn,
> your hands cracked from milking,
> you let me help you rub in mutton tallow,
> thick and sticky. Nights around
> our homework ended with your knuckles
> rapping, tough, veined, square-nailed, wide.
> "O.K. Bedtime! Hit the sack."

It's my turn now.
Your hands are still.
Did I knock, I wonder,
wanting to surprise you,
wanting one more time to touch?
We said we'd help each other
any way we could. Well, sweet ghost,
it's over. Knock on wood.

Stomping Out the Blues

for my brother, Jess

The night our father died, we danced
our hearts out at the Thunderbird Red Lion
Motor Inn, high on cognac we could ill afford.
The band, a stand-up rock-and-crazy-roll group
with electric yellow hair and hips as thin
as bed slats, wailed into the night,
sequined jackets pushed above their elbows.

Brother, you were jazz-hot, lusty, the way
you used to be in high school when we bopped
to "Rip It Up," and "Ready Teddy"
in the kitchen, making the dishes rattle,
the pans jump. Dad would get up
out of bed, twist his pajama fly
to one side, try to stop us.

Light-headed as helium balloons,
we danced back those years
when we grew up in his house,
glugging sloe gin in the Roundup Grounds,
wiggling our suits off in the swimming pool.
We never fooled him much, a vet
with six of us and all those animals.

Our bones and blood in synch,
both sensing every step and turn,

our maker free now, we let go,
whirling around the burned-out fire.
We raised the dust on that small dance floor,
stomping out the blues, our father's
heart still beating in our restless feet.

The Cowl of Night

on Garden, Ashes, *by Danilo Kîs.*

Andi, the hero's son, too young to understand
the Second World War, his father's disappearance,
    blamed night for biting away
    the old man's brilliance,
for swallowing up his celluloid collars
and other trappings of a wizard dad, conjurer,
        writer, practical joker whose absence
        was the ladder of a railroad track.
In his nightmare dreams, he listened for the dark
to open up its teeth and spit him back,
return him, clickety-clack, in a burst of laughter.

Night also ate my father, crept in while he
was dreaming, slipped a monk's cowl on his head.
    A country vet, he talked to ewes,
    the kerosene lamp making shadows
all night in the lambing shed, casting
a magic shine on each wet lump of life.
        First World War, he broke in horses,
        blinkered mules bound for France.
When he died, we found his hickory-handled
ballpeen hammer hiding behind the curtain, ready
to test the teeth of wild horses. He thought the
willow was the wind, rustling their manes;
he could hear them pawing at his pillow.

St. Grandma the Baptist

Lulu Hofus Belton, 1865-1945

I thought she lived in the promised land.
Her yard, a brown desert with two date palms,
was like a Sunday-school picture. She loved
to hose the birds out of the fronds
at sundown, told us they made a mess
like spilled milk on the sidewalk.

In the backyard, she grew figs in trees
she watered every night. From ladders shoved
into their obscene leaves, she picked
the ripe ones every afternoon. Washing them
first, of course, she laid them out to dry
in a homemade tray perched on gray sawhorses.

Her hair pulled back in a fig-like fist,
she insisted, while we were with her,
that we learn Right from Wrong: keep clean
at all costs; keep regular; be punctual
for meals. Every morning, exactly
as the cuckoo in her clock croaked eight,

she would open her costive face
and yell, "Breakfast's ready!" We'd hurry down
to find her on her prickly chair, three re-hydrated,
plumped-up figs on moistened shredded wheat.
She'd even spit my bangs in place, carrying out
her mission—to baptize everything in sight.

Veterinarian's Daughter

Afterwards we blamed the cat.
    The kittens need a christening;
    bring champagne!
And so he came, excited, never having seen
a birth before, longing for the ritual.
We popped the cork, drank to the firstborn,
mewing already in the cardboard box,
settled for a long watch on the sunroom floor.

Our glasses clinked for every slippery sack
expelled, small tumid sausages squeezed
into the world, again for every afterbirth
licked off.
    Alley whore, experienced, she tidies
    up each trick before the next.
The sticky kittens eased along her body,
nuzzling for nubbins in her hair.

She bore four orange babies in two hours,
and we drained a fifth of Cook's best Brut.
    With cats you can't be sure. There may be
    more. We might find another in the morning.
My nipples itched. My forearm moved
across my breasts, electrified the tips.

As I talked, I moved my hand to his inner thigh,
then up and up, cupping his crotch,
a huge bulge hard against the zipper.

Purring, he pulled me toward him,
his heart knocking, his mouth moist.
I think you've found another one, already.
We skinnied our shirts and jeans off on the floor
and rolled together toward the kittens.

Parrot on Fire

on a photograph
by Christopher Rauschenburg

Across moss steps
leading nowhere,
a knife of light
cuts emptiness in two.
The whetted sun
carves scars
on pavement, on
settled buildings.
Jagged cracks leap
into lightning.

My Uncle Dave,
weird, bearded man
who huffed his breath
onto a stereopticon
and wiped it with his elbow,
lived in rural Iowa,
kept a parrot
in a metal cage.
He believed in miracles.
When a streak of light
burned through
his farmhouse window,
he said, "Look!
That bird's feathers
are on fire!"
And I believed him.

All my life I longed
to own a parrot,
its flaming feathers
burnished gaudy
green and orange,
a hooked brass beak,
sulphurous glassy
eyes. I, too, believe
in miracles: forsythia
drawing yellow flowers
from brown hats;
green moss sprouting
hairs of hammered copper;
the moon, a shave of
lemon in an April sky. . . .

The list is endless:
Rauschenberg;
my Great Uncle Dave;
the mind's eye. . . .

Signal Flowers

A cemetery west of the Wasatch mountains
bakes in the summer sun, brown as leather faces
of old Mormon farmers—
      Ephraim, Jacob, Dan—who lie there:
Father's Day, driving that empty landscape
and thinking of my father, I stop to read
their names.
      (He would have had a horse, here,
erstwhile cowboy, pioneer.)
On a cross back by the corner fence,
hangs a rakish, new, white Stetson hat.
Beneath it, in the dust,
      a dozen fresh-cut, blood-red gladiolus.

*

By the empty house of Rilke's childhood
at Fruili, in a garden long abandoned, he found
the stone among the grasses
      where he and Amelia, his first sweetheart,
played. A fresh bouquet of violets lay upon it,
      framed by heart-shaped leaves.
How could flowers appear from nowhere? Rilke felt
some ghost hand must have sent them,
      blown on the winds of early May,
or couched in the falling dew.

*

Here beside the ocean, a few nasturtiums
splashing orange on the cedar fence,
the roar of water makes the porch
            a trap for angels' voices.
They oscillate from clouds like tailless kites
buffeted by weather.
    The spring after my young husband died,
pear boughs the wind had broken off
sprinkled blossoms along the walk,
            showing me the way,
        asterisks of stars beneath my feet.

Going Underground

The way you can't see what's ahead,
or how the wind is blowing
in a car, the top down,
driving at top speed,
hair lashing across your eyes
like cobwebs, the memory
of my mother, ten years dead,
    fuzzes out of sight.

The last time I was home,
I went with pussywillows
to her grave,
read the names on stones
I thought were close to hers,
found the tree I'd lined up
with a mountain peak as snow fell
    on her last flowers.

Circling that well-remembered place
for nearly an hour, hunting,
I could not find the marker.
A dimple in the lawn
dropped me to my knees,
brushing back her hair,
tearing away the grass
    that hid her face.

To Other Worlds

Sören Matsen, 1888-1983

There, above the gorge,
where winter winds rivaled anything
that blew in off the fjords,
the Danes who settled Washington
had need of resolution.

To that high and God-spurned land
men came, despite the burning cold,
the spring-thaw flood, carrying three
necessities: a hammer forged in Europe,
a wife, and a cast-iron aebelskiver pan.

The rest they carried in their blood.
For eighty years, one uncle
dry-farmed wheat, grew everything
the family ate, fixed the battens
on the barn, and helped his neighbors harvest.

Honest, hard-working, he was frugal
as a hungry hen. He never owned
a bathrobe. Wittenburg was beyond
his schooling, but his word was law,
his handshake truer than a paper, signed.

His last request was softer than the earth
he'd worked. They honored it with malt
and home-cured meat; with him, they buried,
in one hand, his old hammer,
in the other, a sheaf of ripened wheat.

Different Albums

Michael Peter Middlehurst, 1930-1979

You paused in the gravel
under the streetlight,
    raised your two hands up
in front of your face
as if taking a picture,
        clucked your tongue
for the shutter's click,
    turned on your heels
without a word
and crumped away.

It was so like you,
that brief pantomime,
    your green eyes alight
with "the divil itself,"
as Mummy Midd would say.
        Even as you left
I wanted to keep your spirit,
    to fill our days
with laughter and
your Irish wit.

I stayed, framed there
inside the gate we'd
    nearly worn the hinges off

those years we lived
beside the Millrace,
          sorry for our hard words,
tilting my head the way
     you used to mimic, saying
you actually preferred
the lopside of my face.

It was the last time
I would see you,
     a moment sharper
than any photograph.
When I heard you had died
          so unforeseeably,
I wanted to call you back
across the gravel to erase
     those last deft gestures,
do a retake, starting
long before you left.

Dawn Wind

Lurah Slocum Sackett, 1926-1988

I wanted to tell you, when we got home
from Spain, about the sunflowers,
   how they turned their faces
      toward the sun like curious children.
They would have reminded you of three-year-olds,
your nursery school charges.
   I wanted you to see them, Lurah,
field on field, bending—
      but you were gone,
    dear secret-sharing friend,
    gone like the summer wind
      into the sky.

Walking in your woods one summer,
the stir of air rustling in the trees,
   we stopped beside the creek
    to watch the alder leaves
floating on the water.
Leaning on that weathered rail, comfortable
with silence, the metaphor informed us.
   We talked lazily, then, being alone,
     of our parallel lives,
     of what, when the kids were grown,
     we meant to do—weave, build a kiln,
       travel, write. . . .

Here, it is the time of spiders.
Their webs in every breezeway
    quiver with your breath, dear spirit,
      your suspiration in the air.
How fragile the fine-spun webs. The spider
waits for a break in that intricate emptiness....
    Dawn wind stirs outside
the open window of my study, billowing
      the eyelet edges of white curtains
        toward me. The sweet breeze
      lifts the edges of my paper,
        Lurah.

Winter Wake for My Brother

Robert Reid Belton, 1923-1992

That last morning,
in your outrageous bathroom
papered with *New Yorker* covers,
I looked beside the mirror
at a goat, his bearded mouth
cat-whiskered with wild
flower stems—yellow
dandelions among the daffodils,
(ridiculously red and blue,)
gentian primroses
low among the tulips.
In the burgeoning light
he stood there, staring,
horny and wide-eyed,
amused, broad-browed above
a quizzical expression.

Since 1967, until you glued
him on the wall, that goat
had followed you around,
waiting for resurrection,
delirious with joy
in spring-fresh sun and air,
the look of caught surprise.
He looks so much like you,
Bob, a felicitous memorial
in grubby clothes,

cloven-hoofed in cracked
and mud-caked shoes,
picking blue delphinium
or happily staking lilies
in your garden—
probably next April.

III

At the Edge of the Land

Drink of the Cup

The taste of that tin cup
stays in my mouth,
the lip of metal rolled
like a hem on linen.
It hung from a nailed stake
for anyone to use, oozing
bloodrust from the seams.

The spring to which he'd taken me,
deep in the woods
somewhere in Iowa heat,
was round as ringworm,
not stained with gentian violet
as my friend Amy's hands had been,
but green and spongy,
inebriant as Lenten lilies.

Thinking about her,
about being afraid to touch her
that time we watched
a river-dunking preacher
wade into the water
with his shoes on,
and drinking from that cup,
it seemed the taste of tin
was both adulterous and holy,
the way his voice squelched
through our childhood,
dripping sin.

The Harvester

Indian-summer naked, we ran at dusk
among the rows of grain tasselling above us,
hiding and seeking, the Iowa earth
still sun-warm on our feet,
our hair dishevelled by the gusts of rain.
Memories spill over me, hoppers
of new-shucked corn, cob and silk alike,
from those foddered days.

Winter-still and green, McCormick-Deering
lived out in the barn where we could play.
We rustled in the sheaves, rejoicing,
as they sang in Sunday School.
Even now, I hear the double name
of that old harvester in Father's mouth,
on the party line, planning the harvest work:
equipment, place, crew, rate, and time.

Late in summer, crouching in a gray-board cave
among Purina stock-feed bags and harness tack,
I hid between the burlap sacks tied
like donkey's ears. From the haymow,
I had eavesdropped on loud-mouthed men
from other counties, huskers, hog-callers,
sorghum-grinding, lye-and-cracklin'-soap-making
neighbors, and blushed to hear them fart
and swear, gearing up to move that big machine.

They spoke of butchering hogs, wells drilled,
axle grease; laughed and slapped each other
on the back, swore at Roosevelt's Relief.
Then it was done. The engine fired.
The door slid open to reveal my hiding place.
"What're you up to, Missy?" some farmer cried.
Then, softening, said, "You want a ride?"
That mechanized grotesque squeaked into motion,
heading for the uplands in the sun.
From the big McCormick-Deering,
I could see the foxes run.

Point of No Return

Mother soaked her menstrual rags
in cold water, in an old enamel canner
in the basement. It stayed empty
down there by the washtubs
through the month, chipped past
its intended use, the blue glaze
from years of heat cracked on the bias,
rusting in strings like torn beef jerky.

Once, when I was twelve and brinking
onto instinct, mother was sick.
Unusual for her, she stayed in bed
all day. Standby helper, oldest
daughter of her six, having dressed
the younger boys to play in snow,
I started down the stairs to get our sled.

Instead, I found my father, his sleeves
rolled up above his elbows, his arms
immersed in scummy, pinkish suds,
the water in the tubs, sloshing.
In one half of the galvanized sink
the washboard slanted, a bar of brown
Fels-Naptha at the top, a heap of rags
wrung out like twists of taffy
at the bottom. In the other rinse,
more stained squares—bits of old
sheet blankets, torn dishtowels, gauze—
like drowned fish, floating.

I slowed down, mid-way. I must have known,
by some presentiment another month
would prove, what he was doing:
that few men bent to such blood sacrifice
except through guilt, great relief, or need.
He turned, caught unawares, straightened
to authority and said, too sharply,
unforgettably, "Go back, *now*!
Do you hear? Get back up those stairs!"

Heartwood

Late April, dodging rain spots on my lens,
I swim in milkglass air to capture etchings, exquisite
outlines of large-hearted trees not yet in leaf.
      Small brown sparrows, starlings, chicadees
lace through the limbs, chirping down the sky.

The trees hold still. They comfort me, these
steadfast testaments to patience, their girths
of deep-grooved bark and vaulted crowns slow-breathing.
      Rooted layers down, they wick water
from so deep they pull primeval time up into air.

From my dwarfed perspective, I salute them,
jot their names down on an envelope. Suddenly, the list
becomes an old dance card, catkins for the tassels.
      Twirling and circling, we embrace—Sequoia,
Tulip Poplar, Elm, Oak, Copper Beech....

All thirty-six exposures click off quickly
in the energy of sap-rise. My palm-sized automatic whirs,
rewinding. The slight vibration scrolling backwards
      is the universal dream of seeds, to hum a
synchronous pulsing up through hearts of trees.

Beside a Desert River

Here, in the shade of junipers,
the desert full of smell and sound—
sage and greasewood, sun-dried grass,
the red-winged blackbird's call—
you have come back whole to me,
my first love, beside a river
purling through tall reeds, where
marsh wrens scold and rapids
roil the muddy water, mirage
created by sweltering weather.

You have come to this palpable air,
this emptiness, chimerical as heat waves,
to surprise me here, with students
the same age we were when we marked
our broad-jump records in the desert dust
with broken juniper boughs,
the berries acrid, reeking like cat pee.

We have kept our ears cocked
all this musky afternoon, eyes
peeled for rattlesnakes, tracks
of coyotes, arrowheads in the sand.
Across the Blixen river, a prairie falcon
poses in the rocks, stiff as taxidermy.
Here, where desert brightness
sears away pretenses, I miss
your vibrant life. The clouds
are changing patterns on the land.

Conjugal Ghost

Under the canvas umbrella, I sit
with casaba rinds and muffins. Sunday
morning. You sneak back, hungry to talk.
What can I say to you,
hovering beside me in this blue cocoon?
Can you smell the spicy petunias,
these *Comanches,* red enough to shout?
I know you cannot answer,
now—your mouth empty, your eyes out—
but my tongue still forms a conversation
with you, Johnny,
the way nerve memory
twitches in a severed limb.

*

Heat creeps up under the table
through these metal holes,
breathes an exhalation of dry grasses,
the end of August.
Our children are inside;
their children splash like otters
in the plastic pool. (Two look like you,
their blonde hair bleached in streaks,
their eyes back-lit and clear.)
I will sit out here awhile
to watch the locust leaves
stir with each slight puff of air,

the ripple of light on lime-green
napkins. Yellow jackets,
      nervous as memory,
hover over bacon crumbs.

           *

    I went to our high-school reunion.
I sat in the bleachers where you gave me
your letterman's sweater.
        Duane and I danced
to "String Of Pearls," "Frenesi."
Flop is bald. Jack wore a white linen suit;
he sells insurance.
    I kept thinking you were there.
Time passes, that's all. The flit of memory—
summer picnics,
        those times I'd cut
a melon for our breakfast, put a spoon
of sugar in your coffee.

Short Rations

In a Canadian Pacific diner between Winnipeg
and Saskatoon, a woman lurches toward us
to sit down. Her husband, hands strong
as milking stools, steadies her. His hair
is tufted prairie grass, but she is frail,
her eyes as pale as blue skimmed milk.

They find the menu, glad for something hands
can do, and study choices, his eyes on the price,
hers on all that food. Then he orders—bran
muffins, two apiece. "Without butter," he adds
gruffly, "and bring her Ladyship some tea."

Wanting to ease a nervousness I sense
between them, I praise the texture of her
thick, tweed coat. She stares at me, as if
she dare not answer. My voice frees him,
instead, to speak. Starved to talk,
he rasps out stories—

        of bleakness on the land, homesteading
        in the Territories fifty years ago,
        winters he'd had to string a rope
        between the house and barn, blizzards
        so hard they blinded horses,
        the coming of "electric" to the farm,
        selling eggs to Indians, driving
        the buckboard wagon into town.

I ask if they are going to visit children.
"*She* never had any...." He jerks his head
in her direction. She adjusts the napkin
on her lap. When the muffins come and he stops
talking, she leans her body toward me,
fingering her sleeve, her voice an echo
from some cave within. She whispers,
"I got this coat before I married *him*."

In the Waterfall Garden: Seattle

Across a smooth-lipped ledge,
the garden's waterfall unreels
yards of finished satin, threaded
with the filaments of snowmelt.
Light slivers through split-leaf maples,
the needles of Tanyasho pine,
glossing the fluent folds, ess-ing
in figure eights like honey.

Facing it, a wall of rock, adamant
and dry as August, coughed up hot
and pocked by earth's deep bubbling
geologies ago, once formed the ribs
of the Sierras. The stone is blood-
brown, impervious to moss or fern spores,
whiskerless as an ancient shaman
squinting in the desert.

In this miniature garden
in the city where you live, I watch
the fall of water, the thirsty stone.
Refracted color sparkles through the mist.
Where the backwater forms a quiet pool,
tubs of periwinkles bloom. There,
two dragonflies are buzzing,
dizzied by each other's iridescence.

At Walden Pond

This wilderness of bright birch, maple,
quenched the thirst of one who tracked
his spirit's journey like a hunter,
watched for signs of fox and muskrat,
deer scat in the snow. October scatters
leaves across the surface of the pond.
Around the edge, trees fold out,
flaming in the water. Thoreau once
dipped his wooden bucket here.

Bent down to the lapping edge alone,
like Old Nakomis on the shore,
or Yeats beside his lake on Innisfree,
I trail an elusive etch in water.
What deity of history lingers in this
place? From the gravel where he bent
to crack the ice, to skim pure water,
an echo urges, "Simplify, simplify."

Crows argue. Fish rings pock-mark
the intervals of silence. Both priest
and acolyte, I dip my hand into the sacred
spring, touch my forehead, then my lips,
as if some ritual would bless me.

As fish gall once in Nineveh scaled film
from Tobit's eyes, so this holy water clears
my vision for a glimpse of inner landscape
and the pathway through it, a simple trail
that praises nature at each turning.

Call the Interval Happiness

Only yesterday, dear Susan, did I learn
of your hard journey just beginning.
Having stared at the care you took
to calligraph the Stafford lines,—
"Even pain you can take, in waves:
call the interval happiness."—
I somehow knew.

Admiring your clean art, I stood there,
heard your pen strokes pray for strength,
scratch at the door that opens on some core
of energy you now must draw from.
And I knew your choice of what to write
had not been random.

Only cells are random, sometimes,
those that you, whose world is ordered
beauty, now must battle. The chaos
in your body breaks my heart.
It is an irony that begs for bitterness,
but you refuse.

Outside my study window, the leaves
of late October fly from the trees,
and ivy vines, their ligneous tendrils
summer-strong, wrap around the bark.
I look for words with arms of love
to wrap around you, now.

Instead, you take my hand, guide it
with your own, the way a poem of Bill's
will lead us gently on. It is a gift
you both have, this patient knowing
that art can open pathways
through the dark.

Wheat Harvest

Dusk. A low sun fire-red from chaff and straw and dust.
The combines push to cut the day's last swath,
    herringbones across the land.
In all directions under haze, the wheat fields stretch
in gentle swells, an afghan of brown trouser patches
    pieced together, too hot for this August season.
They kick the covers off, these sweaty big machines.

> *My hands move across my knees, mounds*
> *that fit the palm's curve, the hills,*
> *the dunes of wheat, as if those rounds were*
> *breasts or bottoms, loaves of fresh-baked bread. . . .*

From my parked car, I watch the lumbering hulks.
The dust of harvest settles on the windshield
    like sunbaked varnish on old shiplap,
flaking off and sloughing down the glass.
The diagonal phalanx of dinosaurs munches its way
    through thigh-high grain,
the way the teeth of clippers shave a boy's thick hair.

> *It will grow back. I smile. As will the grain*
> *next year. Yes. Just that. It is incipience*
> *that holds me here, the promise of renewal,*
> *the seminal pulse of more than wheat,*
> *away and beyond the limits of our knowing. . . .*

The nervous sickle cuts across the stalks;
paddle wheels turn like steamboats on the river—

thwack, thwack, thwack, lifting the grain
onto slow conveyors. The chaff is blown away;
the wheat collects in sensuous swirls like honey.
　　Held in awhile, that hummock of harvest gushes
through swiveling chutes into the empty trucks
lying alongside, waiting to be filled. . . .

> *My muscles tighten, that last push delivering*
> *a baby. I am holding that slippery body on my belly,*
> *tearful with relief that it is whole, all its life*
> *ahead and I as witness, watching new yeast rise.*

Widower

Late summer nights, he'd light a candle
at his open window to invite the moths.
Perhaps she would be there, the white one,
his wife come back.
                The stars
were not more white,
nor the milk in the pan.

He sat a long time beside her when she died,
feeling her hand grow cold. Her spirit
finally flew, he told us, to the wall
above her bed,
                a single moth
with round, brown eyes
and nightgown wings.

We took our dear friend produce
from the garden, an excuse to talk,
suggested, finally, he come with us
to some place
                away from home,
some place he'd never been.
One day he agreed.

At Mycenae, that next summer, we waited
in the shade of the Lion Gate, impatient,
as he stumbled over stones in glaring sun
to photograph
                white butterflies,
thinking she was with him
smelling the wild thyme.

Evening Light

The wind rises. Fog blows off the water.
Tomorrow, the low tide of the year,
we will get up early, to see the feathery anemones
    like underwater flowers in the tidepools,

to marvel at the multi-colored starfish
plastered to the underside of rocks,
to search for ancient chitons, small deflated footballs
    stuck like suction cups below the waterline.

We want to watch the birds that nest on Haystack,
the guillemots who scavenge hermit crabs
venturing from their borrowed mollusk shells,
    the hooked-nose puffins, their beaks like embers

on a plump cigar, pumping their pudgy wings
to stay aloft, the cormorants who coast to rest,
then brake, heels first, to slap wet wings
    like Batman's cape against the rocks to dry.

The hum goes on, here at the edge of the land.
The sea mumbles. The crow scolds from the hemlock,
and the dog next door, tired of chasing seagulls,
    crunches dry dog food on the porch.

We go on too, my love, trying to deny change,
now, though changing, keeping a sharpened eye
on changes, adjusting the curtains
    to catch the evening light.

Jane Glazer grew up in a large family in rural Iowa, among animals and books. Widowed at thirty, she raised three children, earned an M.A. in English literature from the University of Oregon, went to Dublin, Ireland, as a Fulbright scholar, and spent two years in the Peace Corps in South America. She has taught for nearly twenty years in Eugene and Portland, most recently at Catlin Gabel School. Currently, she is an urban forestry commissioner in Portland, Oregon, where she lives with her architect husband.

Some Trick of Light has been designed and produced by John Laursen at Press-22 during the spring and summer of 1993. The type is Stone Serif, and the paper is acid-free Starwhite Vicksburg Archiva. The cover image is a gouache and water-color painting by Richard Morhouse, entitled "West."